THE VOICE OF
BENMOD TheEvolvingSpecies

*Thoughts, ideas, views, and opinions
to help you manage yourself in life*

Benson N. Modie
B.Sc., M.Phil., Ph.D.

BENMOD
TheEvolvingSpecies

Promoting human effectiveness

I dedicate this book to the human species;

HOMO SAPIENS

Listen to Understand
and
Read to learn more!!

ThePerfectLEARNINGApproach

Acknowledgements

This book owes its existence to the numerous seminars and workshops on human resources and work improvement I went through, while an employee of the Botswana Department of Geological Survey. I am particularly grateful to Stephen Hacker (The Performance Centre), who at one of such workshops posed the question *"What are you here for?"*, to me and others. This question led me into becoming more aware of several possibilities to contribute to life, including some of the ideas shared in this book, and ultimately I created my own vision document for the future I desire. I am also greatly indebted to the many colleagues, friends, as well as many of the world's personal development teachers I have been exposed to through their books, audio's etc., whose wisdom and inspiration has been instrumental to my motivation. Many thanks go to my colleagues Professor Read Mapeo and Dr. Nelson Toteng, who kindly agreed to read and evaluate the manuscript of this book. Lastly, I would like to express my gratitude to the media in general for bringing me a bird's eye view of the scene that is modern human life-styles, which allowed me to generate the many opinions shared in this book.

Copyright © 2012 Benson N. Modie

The Centre for Knowledge
P. O. Box 1382, Lobatse
Tel: +267 7162 4001
Email: tesbnm@gmail.com

All rights reserved. No part of this book may be reproduced or transmitted in any form or by any means, electronic or mechanical, including photocopying, recording, or by any information storage and retrieval system, without permission in writing from the publisher.

ISBN:1477455760

Dear friends,

This book is the result of four decades of learning, during the first-half of my life, when I discovered that *"the power of knowledge is to create the future I desire"*. During this period I learnt how to learn, in other words, how to acquire knowledge, and then how to use that knowledge to create the future I desire. Today I am in early days of the second-half of my life, and I consider myself a new elder. My strongest desire now is to share the knowledge I have acquired this far with others, and this book therefore is created to fulfil just that.

Below is a brief history of how it all started. At the beginning of the seventies decade I went to a primary school that had a badge labelled *"knowledge is power"* but then I failed to master the meaning of the phrase. Nevertheless, the *"knowledge is power"* phrase was inscribed into my subconscious mind, and decades later it grew to become part of the conscious mind, and subsequently I discovered the power of knowledge. Four years before the beginning of the twenty-first century, at a Time Management seminar, I was offered a book authored by Kerry Gleeson titled *"The Personal Efficiency Programme"*. From this book I learnt a simple but effective skill, which though it was meant to improve office work-practices, I found greatly helpful for the management of self in life. This simple skill involves noting down all the ideas or thoughts that come into your mind whenever and wherever so that you do not forget them, for some may be very useful at a later stage. On reading other motivational and inspirational literature I got to learn that this simple skill helps in thought analysis and allows for the recognition of your inner-self or true-self desires. I got my first personal notebook in 2003 to record my thoughts, ideas, opinions, and views, and since then I have several of such notebooks. In this book you will learn about these thoughts, ideas, opinions, and views, and I hope you will find something useful that will make you too realize the power of knowledge.

The book is arranged following the chronological order of the personal notebooks to demonstrate the trends and frequency of occurrence of common thoughts, which reflects my dominant desires and passions. In other words, for the individual, the ideas that keep coming back to his/her mind, in thoughts, are often a reflection of his/her true-self desires in life, and hence needs careful attention. This book is simply a mixed bag of my thoughts over time which I documented and analysed, and eventually recognized my true-self desires. Ultimately, I was able to construct my preferred vision of life on the basis of these thoughts, and I believe that you too can do the same in your life.

Once, at a Performance Management seminar, in 2001, I was asked what I consider to be such an intriguing question. The question was "*why are you here?*" and the answer it sought was in another question of the form "*why are you here in this life on earth? Or what is your purpose for being?*" In three years since I was asked this question I wrote down the first draft of my own purpose. Today I find that preferring activities that help fulfil my purpose gives meaning to my life, and this has become a pillar for my self-management in life. I believe that you too can learn a little something from this experience and be able to create meaning in your life as well as the future you love to experience.

I created this little book to fulfil my purpose through sharing what I believe has potential to help others to understand their true-selves and to begin to consciously create their own preferred future. It is always better to share what little idea you have with others whilst still in life than to have those ideas end-up at the graveyard.

Kind regards,

Benson N. Modie

Foreword

I wish for the emergence of a human species centred on its Spirit, loving and protective to life, with a much improved brainpower to only focus on empowering and productive thoughts that are life-saving.

This is a book motivated by the endless struggles portrayed by modern human-life styles, despite the fact that we humans consider ourselves to be the most sophisticated and well-advanced species ever. Some even believe that we are the ultimate in all of nature creations, and that everything that exists was meant for humans. However, the world today is inundated with human activities that contradict the view that humans are the most advanced amongst all living species.

All around the globe we see daily conflicts ranging from the scale of wars between and among nations to community and family tragedies that have resulted, and still continues, in the destruction of life for the human species by the human species. Elsewhere around the globe great minds, so it is believed, gather at major high-level technological meetings on defence and security, the aim being to design the most effective weaponry for security and defence. What this means though in simple language is to design a weapon precise enough to make sure that life is terminated with no chance for survival. This is just one among numerous world-wide activities that humans engage in, which look set to halt human evolution or equally accelerate human extinction. Modern man alone is succeeding in polluting the environment, in which also lives other species, and hence poses a great risk to all that is life on Planet Earth. Nations, communities and organisations in many parts of the world continue to struggle to develop effective structures and systems that can allow for a long-term enhancement of the quality of life for all. This is despite the numerous and costly developmental initiatives and work reform processes introduced at different levels of human organisational settings. Does this reflect the highest level of operation of the human brain in terms of developing thoughts to secure and sustain life for the human species? Is the human species developing or deteriorating? If we take the human species away from the domain of the material world, largely considered as indicative of development and success, and view him in his natural form, can we say the human being is developing to become a better species?

The concerns and questions above are what the author of this book, Dr. Benson N. Modie, often found his mind engaged on, as he observed the struggle that humans undergo on Planet Earth. Ultimately, Dr. Modie developed the zeal to share these concerns and offer possible solutions.

In this book you will find several discussions on many issues of human life as well as opinions and suggestions on possible solutions to many of life's everyday problems. The book puts more emphasis on the process of learning, to acquire knowledge, and the need to proactively respond to knowledge gained, by acting/ using the knowledge and skills acquired during the learning process, to meet human life needs. This book emphatically addresses people at their individual level, and encourages them to embrace the learning process, in order to expand their knowledge base, so as to improve the quality and value of the decisions they make on a daily basis, both at work and in life in general. A core element of this book is the subject of personal development for individual effectiveness and overall management of self in life. The objective is to influence individuals to upgrade and enhance their own worth and become invaluable components of the system that is human-life and its major drivers e.g. family, workplace, and community settings. The discussions in the book are designed to influence everyone to challenge/interrogate themselves with regard to their own involvement and contributions in life, as well as to develop a much more broader picture of life beyond just the local environment.

The book offers a wide variety of topics that includes issues on education, politics, wellness, religion, personal fulfillment etc., in order to create the opportunity for many people to take part in the discussions. An interesting feature of the book is the arrangement of the discussions in a sequential order, following the dates during which such mind discussions were undertaken. This is a feature deliberately created to make individuals aware of their thought patterns, and ultimately develop awareness and a clear picture of the issues that dominate their thoughts. The latter are commonly the burning issues for individuals which when acted-on, positively and effectively, allows for much improvement in the quality of life as well as personal effectiveness and productivity of the individual concerned. This mind-mapping procedure is a very attractive and powerful tool in the formulation of personalized projects, which have a huge potential for success, due to the build-up of inwardly sourced personal motivation.

INTRODUCTORY HIGHLIGHTS

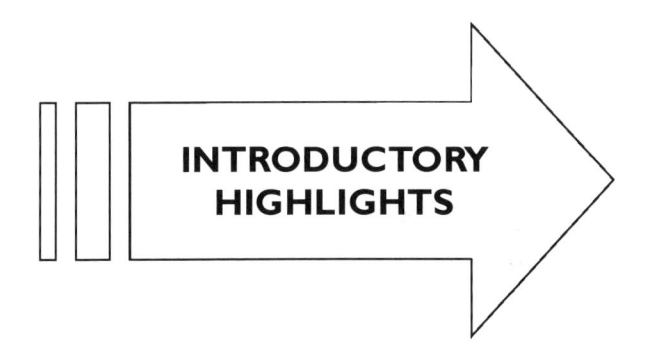

The only real success in life is the attainment of the conditions of peace, love, joy, and happiness.

MY TEACHINGS
⇒ 11. 03. 06

What I teach and share is nothing new but mostly the same old story! You have heard much of this before from your parents, peers, community leaders, the authorities at school or workplace or health centres, your national leaders, as well as from a diverse array of world authorities. The question though is "Have you registered any of this as knowledge? And are you using it in deciding upon your daily choices in life?". My teachings are based on the concept of "*eldership*", which involves the sharing of knowledge from experiences in life. Such knowledge was amassed from the above list of learning forums. It is very important for all individuals to create and raise their awareness and consciousness levels at all times, to allow for maximum benefit in knowledge acquisition from such forums. The benefits of such an approach will be expanded knowledge base, growing whole, effective self-management in life, and ultimately a sure possibility in creating happiness and joy in life.

STEP IN EVOLUTION
⇒ 19. 03. 06

My teachings are aimed at helping people to manage themselves well in life, so that ultimately we can, as the human species, attain a step up the ladder of evolution. I have learnt from the subject of Palaeontology that the development and evolution of living species require a favourable condition of life. Hence, I believe that with us humans such a favourable condition can only come about if we desist from anti-life habits and begin to manage ourselves effectively in life. My idea of a step in evolution does not suggest the emergence of a five-eyed being or one with wings or anything of that magnitude. Instead, I envisage the birth of a species centred on its spiritual-self, loving and protective to life, with a much improved brain power to only prefer productive and useful thoughts that are life-saving. Such will be a species that does not struggle with ego-driven devilish thoughts that works against life's continuity. This is my biggest wish for the human species.

BENMODTheEvolvingSpecies
⇒ 21. 05. 06

I believe that as a species we are focusing on the wrong target for our continued existence, and thrive, on Planet Earth. Much emphasis is on the world of wealth and related products. We need to re-focus and put emphasis on species development, i.e. personal growth, to attain a step in evolution.

BENMODTheEvolvingSpecies
⇒ 21. 06. 06

I believe that life for the human species, like any other living species, has to be nurtured through the creation of a favourable niche for survival. My own preference in creating such a niche is to build a foundation of knowledge upon which the decisions on choices for living life are based on.

INFLUENCING WORLD DEBATES
⇒ 23. 06. 06

The Evolving Species that is me hopes to influence the world to behave and act in a way that would help preserve and prolong life on Earth, this in fulfilment of my purpose for being. Today the world is inundated with life threatening and destructive events such as conflicts, terrorism etc. World debates by the powerful of this world unfortunately also focus on using weapons of life destruction to try and stop such life-destroying acts. I would prefer instead an approach that uses life-constructive means.

To develop such a means would call for a major research-based investigation, world-wide, of the same scale as that employed in developing sophisticated weapons, space programmes etc. Such an investigation would be aimed at mapping out the root causes of all forms of unrest in the world and the preferred solutions by the local people. Then the world can spend resources on implementing these solutions in a life-constructive way e.g. effective education etc. The focus and vigour shown in space programmes, and weapons of mass destructions, should be diverted to such a new approach to help the human species to become better organised and avoid life-destructive events.

NEW ELDER BEN MODIE
⇒ 25. 06. 06

My role is to encourage others to acquire knowledge through learning, for the purpose of effectively managing themselves in life, in order to generate a state of happiness for themselves and their relations. My wish is to have everyone's life anchored on the pillar of knowledge at all times. When you have knowledge i.e. knowledgeable, you know what to do to create your happiness. This would be in contrast to the common situation where most expect to generate happiness in their lives on the basis of wealth accumulation or the material world. Knowledge allows you to understand that you can always choose to be happy at any time you so wish, irrespective. In encouraging others with the practical aspects of life, I prefer to refer to my own experiences that have yielded good results for me rather than just teach what I learned from reading. I personally read widely and put that knowledge into practice, and then share my experiences with others.

BENMODTheEvolvingSpecies
⇒ 16. 08. 06

I believe that it is in the best interest for human development if all people were to rid themselves of blame, hate, arrogance, discrimination etc. etc. It may sound an obvious point, which everyone comprehends, but the reality is that, practically, the majority of people live their lives oblivious of this view, and even care less. However, it is my conviction that to become effective as a species we need to continue learning, teaching, coaching, encouraging etc., and still recognise our varied opinions, views as well as our physical aspects. It is even more important to do so when working with younger persons, so that they can learn the habits of the effective species much earlier and grow with them to yield a new breed of the human species.

BENMODTheEvolvingSpecies
⇒ 11. 09. 06

I believe that my mission, whose aim is to develop purpose-driven individuals, will help people to become self-motivated rather than depend on external factors for their motivation.

MY TEACHINGS
⇒ 05. 02. 07

The intention is to make people aware (self-awareness) at all times about their reason for existence or purpose. Whenever you engage in whatever activity determine whether that fulfils your purpose for being or not. If, for example, you condemn, criticize, blame, abuse etc., does this fulfil the reason of your existence? Could this be what you were created for?

MY TEACHINGS: THE THEME
⇒ 03. 03. 07

It is important not to forget that you are not going to exist on Earth in your bodily human form forever. So, before your time to leave comes you ought to have done what you came here to do. The question then is "Do you know what you came to do?" In other words, what is your purpose for being?

THE VOICE OF THE EVOLVING SPECIES
⇒ 07. 10. 07

The only thing I am asking is for you to, firstly, continue learning to acquire knowledge, and secondly, be responsive to knowledge and create the future you desire. Effective living simply means creating the future you desire and enjoying the experiences there-from, in fulfilment of your purpose for being.

Know that the higher purpose of going through the schools is not a certificate or qualifications to find a job, rather, it is to learn the basic skills and to acquire knowledge to manage yourself well in life!!

**THE VOICE OF
MY TRUE-SELF**

Education is a system of transformation through the learning process to produce individuals that are knowledgeable and pro-active in creating positive conditions of living

GROWING OLD OR GROWING WHOLE?
⇒13. 09. 05

At birth, our brains are like a new computer with empty storage space for digital data. On growing-up we accumulate knowledge that is stored in our brains. The brain continually develops or upgrades itself on receipt of new knowledge i.e. adapts to new knowledge and conditions, and helps you to cope with new challenges. When no new knowledge is received the brain does not grow or develop further to a higher level i.e. becomes stagnant, and everything about you becomes old, therefore, you have grown old. The process of continued learning i.e. receiving new knowledge throughout life, keeps the brain developing to higher levels (upgrades). Ultimately, your being can be defined not only in terms of an increase in your chronological age or ageing of the physical body (i.e. *growing old*), but equally in terms of an expanded knowledge base and a high level of brain development, and function, which is a sign of *growing whole*.

As an example, consider the old computer of the 80's and 90's operating on DOS, which were fine then, and the much improved, in processing capacity, Windows operated computers in use today. Your brain need to develop from the level of the DOS-operated computer to that of the Windows operated computer, in order to handle today's challenges. The brain will only develop or upgrade itself through new knowledge or the process of Personal Growth. If not, it would still operate at the level of the DOS-operated computer, but in an era of the Windows computer, and hence cannot handle today's life challenges, just as much as the DOS-operated computer would not be functional today. However, in the case of the human being this incapacity to handle challenges results in negative emotions (emotional toxins), such as frustrations, depression etc, which overall generates low levels of health for the individual. The lack of Personal Growth results in the brain sending messages throughout the body to say "*hey mates, we are no longer growing, we are old and dying*", and the whole body responds by rapid ageing and eventual death if not rescued through new knowledge. The receipt of new knowledge or the attainment of a higher level of Personal Growth results in the brain sending messages like "*we are cool, we are doing fine*", and every body part responds positively and lively.

THE WORKPLACE AND PRODUCTIVITY
⇒ 14. 09. 05

The majority of people in employment do not perform to greater levels on their jobs because they are doing jobs they do not like or enjoy. Many people are of the view that nowadays it is nearly impossible to find a job that one really likes and enjoy. To most it seems a mammoth task to survive without a job and hence many stay on jobs they do not like for reasons of money, security etc. This situation usually breeds poor results and low productivity at the workplace due to the lack of passion, motivation, commitment etc. The solution: *"find and do the job you love or love the job you do"*.

BEING BUSY AND IMPATIENT
⇒ 16. 09. 05

What are you busy about? When you are always busy you never pay attention to basics or necessary details. You never can spot the little flags or early warning signs with regard to work or life activities. Being busy is a sign of ego-driven momentum to compete and overcome others in similar life competitions.

When always busy you cannot hear your calling, from your divine-self/spiritual-self/inner-self, because of the overwhelming noise of the busy world. When centred on your spiritual-self there is no need to compete against anyone, and hence, there is an absence of busyness, replaced by calmness, and eventual joyous life.

Busyness and impatience leads to non-desirable conditions and ill-health i.e. road accidents, crime, diseases, un-planned-for pregnancies etc.

THOUGHTS
⇒ 18. 09. 05

Thoughts in your mind determine how your day shall go i.e. whether or not you will feel good or feel bad. Thoughts lead to imagination and visualisation of events. To imagine an event leads to real time emotional experience even though the imaginary event may not materialise. Through the process of thoughts and imagination one can influence how they would feel at any given time or moment of their day i.e. excitement, boredom, fear, frustration etc. Ultimately, you are and act like what your thoughts determine! Positive thoughts emanate from your divine-self, which is your true-self, whilst negative thoughts are a feature of your ego-self. It is important therefore to develop a habit to listen to that little still voice of your inner-self that brews only positive thoughts.

LIFE
⇒ 20. 09. 05

Life is as we experience it daily, it is in its natural form. However, most people wish to change life and make it how they would want it to be! Unfortunately, there is no way such can happen because life is a natural, that which we have no power over its creative genesis. To try to change life is like fighting against life itself and resisting creation, but there is no chance of winning against life. The result of fighting against life is usually frustrations and emotional toxins. Life should be lived as it is and enjoyed rather than despised, and this way would be a sign of celebrating nature's creativity rather than resisting it. To live life better and avoid resisting the processes of nature it is important to organise your plan of living i.e. life plan. A life plan offers individuals the routes to enjoy and celebrate life and avoid having to fight life. You cannot win in a war against life because you are fighting against the same forces of creation that made you; it's an attempt to reverse creation.

WORRYING
⇒20. 09. 05

The process of worrying does not make things happen, it is a sign of being stuck. It uses up energy and results in mental and physical exhaustion. The outcome of worrying is usually frustrations and emotional toxins, which are detrimental to your health and overall wellness. It seems the source of worry is in fear and the lack of trust that you or others can handle life well. Worrying is a state of imagining the worst scenario out of a life situation. Of note though is the fact that the resultant emotional and physical feelings are real, no longer an element of the imaginary world. The brain sends messages from the mind, where the thoughts are brewed, that something is not right, and then the body responds in a state of sadness, sorrow or emotional low. You can learn to overcome worries by connecting with your non-physical inner-self or spiritual-self through attention to your inner-dialogue.

UNEMPLOYMENT AND EARLY RETIREMENT
⇒20. 09. 05

It would be a great gesture if those in employment could retire early, to afford those outside of employment an opportunity to contribute through formal employment. People who have been in employment for a length of time have amassed some experience enough to help them start their own workplace that could employ a few other people. Rather than expect young and inexperienced people to struggle by themselves, to find employment after schooling, we should help them by sharing our experiences. I believe that early retirement is certainly a better choice to help with problems of unemployment. Those in employment should seriously consider unearthing their purposes in life and determine their personal visions, in order to develop purpose-led and vision-led personal projects to work on, outside of formal employment.

THE GOOD LIFE
⇒21. 09. 05

If you want to experience the good life you desire then you have to live by simple and basic principles. For example, if you want something, you first make a plan, then you implement the plan, and only then will you get the results you want. Most people are too busy and impatient to sit and make a plan of their lives and what they desire. Picture this: "You want a house but are too impatient to make the plan of your own desire. Instead you instruct the builders to just build you a house, because a house is what you want. On completion, you move in and find that there is only one exterior door, the toilet is outside, there is no fireplace, the windows are either too large or too small etc. etc., all things you would have preferred otherwise". So, you don't like the house now, and you are furious and frustrated.

The good life involves planning in advance the route you wish to take and the future you wish to create, whether it's about buying grocery, building a house, developing a family etc. etc. People who take the time to plan before creating can be described as *"being at cause"* as opposed to *"being at effect"*, as they are responsible for causing the creation of the future they desire.

A HABIT FOR PERSONAL GROWTH
⇒21. 09. 05

Earlier in life I realised that most kids (my peers then) tended to rebel against parental advice or advice from the authorities. At a later stage I decided to take it as a challenge and see what will happen. In other words, I made it a habit to listen and respect my parents, elders, as well as the authorities e.g.

teachers at schools etc. So far so good, life seems to have progressed well. This resulted in me taking more advice from books, especially motivational and inspirational literature, and ultimately a growing love for knowledge. Similarly, I noticed that there is a tendency at work by most employees to refuse tasks they believe do not fall within their job descriptions. Based on prior knowledge, I decided to happily carry out any work task given with the idea that I would be learning something new, which could become handy or useful in the future. This helped me to develop and maintain an attitude of learning new things all the times. Hence, today I have a great love for educational literature, particularly on basic skills on the management of self in life.

PURPOSE
⇒21. 09. 05

Your purpose for being is not something you can copy or borrow from others, but it comes from within you as an individual. Purpose cannot be debated with others otherwise it is no longer one, because of the input from the outside world. Purpose is purely sourced from your inner-self or your spirit and is independent of the opinions of others. One can seek the opinions of others only after discovering ones purpose, in a bid to develop the route to a preferred destination. If for example your purpose is to experience the beauty of the Victoria Falls, and you want to go there on holidays, you can seek opinion on the best route to get there. However, you do not seek opinion on whether you should visit the Vic Falls or Cape Town. The choice of the Vic Falls is the destination determined by your inner-self, and cannot be changed due to external influence.

WELLNESS
⇒23. 09. 05

People generally never give their wellness, especially physical health, priority until they are down with dis-ease. Only if people could create awareness in terms of the food they eat and clean-up their inside i.e. the colon, would there be a reduction in the burden placed on the body system to fight disease. Eating improper foods result in constipation i.e. prolonged stay of food inside the colon, which then decays to release toxic waste that end up being absorbed by the body system, a process termed auto-intoxication. The latter is a process that entails self-poisoning by the body due to constipation and leads to several ailments and diseases. Auto-intoxication puts a strain on the body's natural elimination and cleansing system and paralyses the security mechanism i.e. the immune system.

The process of auto-intoxication can be avoided through colon-cleansing and introducing proper diet, which would enhance the body's ability to fight against diseases and other ailments by pulling all its resources together.

MISTAKES AS LEARNING POINTS
⇒*23. 09. 05*

Learning is the process of acquiring knowledge. There are various ways of acquiring knowledge, and amongst them is the way of mistakes. Mistakes are learning points which should be considered positively rather than portrayed in a negative way. A mistake is a lesson to the effect that something is better handled another way, than the one employed. People who never make mistakes are those who never do anything i.e. sit and do nothing in life. However, as the saying goes *"things only happen because you make them happen"*, it is imperative that one has to do something in order to take part in life.

RISK
⇒*23. 09. 05*

Taking a risk is the act of taking fear head-on and breaking the barrier of fear to reach your preferred destination. Risk is a condition of uncertainty over the outcome of your actions. It's worth remembering though that taking a risk is making a choice and that you do not have control over the consequences. Hence, you have to have the character of an individual who is *At Cause*, ready to learn from your past and move on.

Equally important to remember is the point that failure to take risks in life is failure to make things happen for yourself.

EDUCATION
⇒23. 09. 05

Education is the process of transformation, through new knowledge acquisition, to become a pro-active and action-oriented individual who creates positive conditions of living. Being educated is the act of using the knowledge you acquired through learning to change a life condition, from its present status to a desired level. Learning is the process used in education to acquire knowledge; it is not equivalent to education, instead it is a process within the broader system of education. It is commonly assumed that those who have been through the education system are educated, however, the actions of most, in terms of use of knowledge in changing conditions of life is to the contrary.

The reality is that most people have gone through the learning process and acquired a certificate, which they consider to represent being educated. However, being educated includes the act of using knowledge acquired, through the learning process, in a visible manner that shows positive growth.

A certificate on the other hand is to a large extent an indication of the ability one has to learn and recall what was learnt, as it is issued commonly following a written exercise, test, exams or some practical exercise based on past training lessons.

MARRIAGE
⇒25. 09. 05

A lasting marriage is one defined by a partnership between two purposeful individuals. Each requires the support of the other to fulfil their life purposes, rather than their neediness and insecurity as is the case in most marriages. Neediness and insecurity can easily result in manipulation of one partner by the other. Purposeful partners understand that the other partner should maintain and live their purpose for being rather than live the other partner's purpose. Partnership in marriage does not mean one partner adopts the other's purpose, for purpose can not be copied or borrowed but instead comes from inside-out, its source is spiritual. To attain lasting marriage it requires that partners not stand on the way of each other due to their own insecurity and neediness.

UNEMPLOYMENT AND ECONOMIC HARDSHIPS
⇒27. 09. 05

Governments, worldwide, have the obligation to properly manage economies for the benefit of all citizens. It is the responsibility of governments, as institutions that manage public resources, to make sure that resources are made available to uplift the lives of all people wherever they reside. Policies should be put in place and maintained to regulate employment in an effort to get everyone a chance to have some form of employment at some stage of their lives.

People in employment, particularly in the public service, should have a limited stay in their positions, in order to pave way for others, especially the young. There is no doubt the rate of unemployment is rising and nearing crisis levels, and hence the available positions should be managed adequately just like the rest of the resources, in order to benefit the rest of the population. It is inconsiderate to have a small segment of the population enjoy more benefits than others and be allowed to continue to do so by virtue of their employment, at the detriment of the unemployed.

THE POWER OF PURPOSE
⇒28. 09. 05

Purpose provides you with meaning and happiness, as defined by you, through your inner-self or spiritual-self. Being on-purpose implies that you only undertake those activities aligned to your purpose, which are meant to achieve your life goals and objectives. Living on-purpose can bring you lasting happiness that does not require approval from other people. If you are doing what you love and care about, and you achieve your goals as planned, and you fulfil your purpose on a daily basis as per your purpose-driven activities, you have all the reason to be happy, without approval from the world around you.

WHY ARE WE HERE?
⇒28. 09. 05

Most see their lives as comprised of growing up from their birth-time through the education system, and then finding a job to make a living and support a family, and that's it! Could that really be all our existence is about? It feels more like there has to be much more than just making a living and family, then period! A couple of decades and that's it? This means we need to search and find a higher purpose in life. The higher purpose is the reason for our being or existence on earth, which answers the question *"why are you here?"* for each individual. Each individual must have a story to share with those coming into life, and those who will come decades after we left, for the sake of continuity and preservation of the human face on earth.

BLAMES, COMPLAINTS ETC.
⇒30. 09. 05

It is amazing how so many people around the world spend most of their time and energy blaming and whining. Ultimately, everyone must have a story to tell, in order to become a new elder and claim a place at the fire i.e. sharing knowledge and experience with the young and those mainly in the first-half of their lives. People should stop complaining and blaming, instead concentrate on what they desire to do, themselves, in order to change the living conditions for the better. When you complain and blame you are only focusing on the contribution of others, what about yours? Everyone has to learn to be proactive and action-oriented rather than remain passive and reactive all the time. Find meaning in your life, through purpose and make great contributions to life, and then write your stories in order to claim your place at the fire.

BUSINESS ON PURPOSE
⇒30. 09. 05

Most people do not know how to run a business on purpose. Businesses are commonly driven by the eagerness to earn money and support an artificial kind of lifestyle e.g. expensive cars, life on the fast-lane etc. However, such a lifestyle is rarely sustainable and will almost certainly kill-off the business as it gobbles up all the profit. In such cases the purpose is not making money either, rather, it is to live a flashy kind of lifestyle. If the purpose was to make money then the profit would be re-invested into the business to allow for growth.

Business, like any other work, needs a defined purpose to drive it to success. You can focus on the service itself that the business provide to its customers, in which case purpose is defined in terms of service. Alternatively, you can focus on the gifts you provide to employees i.e. salary, and to society i.e. community donations etc. Still you could focus on lessons from business development initiatives, utilised to grow the business, and share those with society as your most important contributions in life. The point is: money need not be the only purpose and motivator for running a business!

RATHER EXCELLENCE THAN PERFECTION
⇒30. 09. 05

There is no perfect in life, but only excellence can be achieved. Even if one believes that they have attained perfection, someone is bound to find fault somewhere! The best is to aim for excellence, which means you do the best you can, to the best of your ability, based on the knowledge you have. Life itself was never intended to be perfect, for example, a quick survey over a small segment of society reveals remarkable physical differences between people. Whether considered physically beautiful or ugly we are all in the same life system together, and we all experience body, mind and spirit. Ultimately, our lives, activities we do etc., should not be viewed and judged in terms of perfection, but rather excellence!

KNOWLEDGE
⇒30. 09. 05

How well you excel in whatever you do depends largely on what knowledge you have about what you desire to manifest. Knowledge is the key to the choices you make in life. Knowledge is what you use to make decisions on a daily basis, and to determine the outcomes you desire in life. It is therefore of paramount importance for all to strive for expanded knowledge base, in order to raise the level of excellence in what they do or wish to do in life.

NOT KNOWING THAT YOU DO NOT KNOW
⇒30. 09. 05

This is a very interesting phenomenon that reflects a certain aspect of ignorance. Some people exist in their daily lives never at any time developing a sense of self-awareness or consciousness about the fact that they may not know something. Most such people only focus on that which they know, and argue their cases through life from only that position. Knowing that you do not know is an ingredient for a growing knowledge base because it propels one to a high level of knowledge quest, in order to learn more, and understand more than you already do about any subject matter of interest and useful to you. Being aware and conscious of the fact that you do not know builds an inquisitive and pro-active mind. Ultimately, it is the right attitude for learning, and changing stereotypes and mind-sets!

EDUCATION AS PRACTICE
⇒01. 10. 05

Society abounds with examples where many people are believed educated because they have gone through the learning institutions and obtained a certificate. As stated earlier, a certificate is only an indicator of the potential one has, to learn and recall, whilst education entails the practice of using the knowledge acquired during the learning process to change a life situation for the better.

For example, many lessons have been given on the dangers of "drinking and driving", but still many are killed as a result of "drink-driving". Surely, people have learned, but it is the practice that is lacking, which is a sure indicator that such people cannot be considered educated. Similarly, much information and knowledge has been offered to contain and reduce the rate of HIV infection, but still the practice has to a large extent been a let-down. To be educated requires that we continue the process of learning even after the schools or universities, to attain complete personal growth and a high level of practical knowledge use.

BETTER DOING AND BEING THAN HAVING AND GETTING
⇒02. 10. 05

If you focus on having and getting, like most people do, you only see a lack in your life. People who focus on having and getting are always eager to get more into their life, hoping to achieve happiness thereafter. However, when you finally get or have whatever you have been after, you immediately begin to focus on something else you want to have. The cycle goes on-and-on until death and there is hardly anytime to enjoy your achievement. It is rare to find such kind of people declaring that they are now satisfied with what they have. It seems better to focus on being and doing, which allows you to enjoy who you are now, as well as what you have now. By being, you accept yourself as complete now rather than after you get or have something else you want. By doing, you focus on what you love and care to do, which allows you to live your purpose now.

ARGUMENT
⇒03. 10. 05

An argument is usually an indication of the difference in the level of knowledge between the parties involved. It is usually a sign that one party knows something that the other does not know. A positive aspect is that one party can learn something new from the other. However, most arguments are ego-driven and are therefore meant to prove the righteousness of one party over the other i.e. Win – Lose!

This "need to be right" often masks the positive aspects of learning something new from an argument. It is always better to listen and understand the other view and appreciate the differences in opinion, and see them in the light of varied knowledge foundations.

LOVE RELATIONSHIPS
⇒ 06. 10. 05

It is very important that in a relationship each partner takes responsibility of their own life. Whatever happens, people should avoid blaming their partners, rather they should observe themselves (i.e. pick up the mirror) to determine how they could be contributing to destabilize the relationship. Remember that you can only change yourself but not the other person.

Remember too that you are in the relationship by choice, your choice, therefore it is your responsibility to control and manage yourself. The highest purpose of a relationship is to build love and partnership, and you do not achieve this by blaming your mate. If after taking responsibility of your own actions and still there is no improvement you can make a choice to leave, but with love and not war.

EARLY RETIREMENT
⇒06. 10. 05

I wish to encourage people who have been in employment for a long time to retire early. First they must define and document their reason for existence, and then spend the second half of their lives on purpose, sharing their experiences with the young and those who have not yet found themselves. There are many great lessons one could learn from their employment over the years, and these could form the basis for finding a purpose to live during the second half of life. Purpose in the second half of life could be in the form of educational advice, on the major life topics in society today, such as relationship killings, HIV/AIDS, rural to urban migration, farming and food production, sports development, organisational work practices, politics and governance etc. A fact: education is the only tool that can bring about positive change.

MONEY
⇒ 07. 10. 05

Many people spend much of their time working hard to make money so that they can get whatever they want. However, it always seems like there is not enough money, which makes many appear miserable in life. Money is certainly galore, and what may be lacking is knowledge on how to make some. But the ultimate problem is the fact that many people do not know how to manage their finances once they have some. Most will spend more than they earn and buy fashionable expensive stuff e.g. flashy cars etc, and hence will forever experience shortage.

I find that it is much better if I spend less than I earn to stay clear of debt and avoid emotional toxins. My best buys are books that help me with knowledge on how to manage myself and the money, and hence I do not believe there is a lack of money in life. To most people money is certainly the thing to live for. However, money is not natural but is artificial i.e. man-made, and it can be made and lost at anytime, such that life centred on money remains unstable forever.

BETTER LIFE WITHOUT EXPECTATIONS
⇒ 13. 10. 05

You should not ask what life provides for you, but rather, what you provide for life. This way there is no expectation from life, instead you focus on what you can contribute to life. Life without expectations is the best because there are no disappointments. Apparently, the best way to determine what to contribute to life is by first finding your purpose for being.

LIFE STRUGGLES
⇒ 15. 10. 05

Many people spend their lives struggling to be someone else who the world around them could accept and approve of. What people do not realise is that while you are busy seeking approval from the world around you your own needs are totally ignored. The best way to avoid such struggles in life is to begin by accepting who you are right now, as there is no need to become someone else. You are perfect as you are. It is more important to find your purpose in life, and spend your life on-purpose because there certainly is no chance for struggle when on purpose. Being on purpose involves working for life rather than expecting from life.

LOVE: WHAT IS IT?
⇒ 18. 10. 05

Most people commonly comprehend love from the basis of feelings of attraction to each other. However, these feelings of attraction are usually based on outside appearance and often have little to do with the inner-person. When such people hurry into a marriage relationship such union is often short-lived, as they begin to discover who their partners are at depth.

Love is something that develops over a long period of time, and can be represented by the commitments people have to each other, the trust, the friendly bonds, consideration and dignity in relating to others etc. These qualities can only develop over a period of time, and hence phrases such as "love at first sight" are totally misleading and should not be taken seriously in searching for a partner to build a lasting union.

THE BLAME SYNDROME (AT EFFECT)
⇒ 18. 10. 05

So many people have chosen to live their lives from the condition of being "at effect", and attribute their lack of happiness and meaning in life to others. Testimony to this condition is readily available near where you are e.g. radio talk-shows, newspapers, television, politics, the workplace etc. People have neglected their own roles and detached from their true-selves or inner-selves, and are completely attached to the outside world. None wants to take responsibility of their own lives, actions etc., and when things do not turn out as expected it is always because "so and so" has not acted in order i.e. blame someone else. People should realise that meaning and happiness in their lives will only come-by if they focus first on themselves, and take full responsibility of their own decisions and choices. Instead of complaining, blaming, and finger-pointing, it is better to take action to improve whatever may need to be improved. Blaming (at effect) uses-up tremendous energy, only to antagonize others and most likely result in emotional toxins.

BLAMERS
⇒ 19. 10. 05

Generally, people who blame others are those that never take responsibility of their own actions and lives. Such people are also afraid of making mistakes for fear of being blamed, hence they never do anything except watch on others! This is well captured in the saying "*people who never make mistakes are those who never do anything*". Most blamers are people that never do anything but sit and grumble, and point fingers at those who are trying their best in life, even with minimal knowledge, to do something about their lives and other life situations. Typical societal blames include those against the government, politicians, employees, employers, parents, teachers, partners, sport referees etc. etc. It is amazing how much energy is spent on blaming and complaining which could otherwise be utilised on being proactively creative and doing. It seems better to offer non-conditional advice to others than blame them, and most importantly to take action yourself to improve whatever you consider in need of some improvements.

MONEY
⇒ 20. 10. 05

Money should never be made master in anybody's life, instead money should always remain in the ranks of servant. Unfortunately, most people have elevated money to a "larger than life" status. Money is a man-made tool, and it seems like its introduction was meant to create some sense of order in life with regard to the distribution of basic needs, but has unfortunately become less effective in today's world. The element of money seems to have grown in influence to become the tool for motivation, for human effectiveness, in development and production. It is however beyond doubt that all mankind production and development on earth can be attained without the use of money but only man-power i.e. psychological and physical. Unfortunately, human beings only understand success and their reason for being in monetary terms, and very few are prepared to work for a course without monetary gains. However, life centred on the element of money is very unstable e.g. fluctuating value, inflation, job cuts or retrenchments etc., which all results in a life of turmoil.

BETTER PURPOSE THAN MONEY
$\Rightarrow$ 08. 11. 05

Having a purpose to live for can help you to detach from money, and liberate yourself from the frustrations of not having money in abundance. Purpose becomes the all important thing to die for in your life!

THE DOWNSIDE OF MONEY
$\Rightarrow$ 09. 11. 05

Many people the world-over paints a picture of money being larger than life. Consequently, with unemployment rife, those who cannot find jobs to earn money turn to crime. Real life is today measured in terms of how much money you have, and this creates a wrong impression that to live a good life you must have more money. Surprisingly, those with more money still want to have even more. Unfortunately, the lesson created by this to all people is that money is life itself! It is therefore no surprise when many people engage in criminal activities, including major conflicts, in order to attain some financial might. Spending lavishly and extravagantly entices the young into wanting to live such life styles, and they resort to crime for shortcuts, since no jobs are available to support such a life style.

OPINIONS
$\Rightarrow$ 31. 12. 05

Opinions are a reflection of individual's interpretation of what they see or perceive, based on their knowledge base. There is no right or wrong opinion but just different opinions, however, people with a need to be right often label other's opinions as wrong. Those with a need to be right will often engage in argument to defend their opinions as right. Such people are rigid and non-flexible in their thinking, and will often miss out on opportunities for learning something new.

Stephen R. Covey (*author*: *7 Habits of Highly Effective People*) suggests that people should "*seek first to understand then to be understood*". In other words, understand first the interpretations of the other person, and then explain your own interpretations about a situation of concern. Opinions can build or break relationships i.e. family, work, politics etc.

PURPOSE
$\Rightarrow$ 04. 01. 06

Purpose is a contract between you (your true-self/spiritual-self) and life. It is what you promise to be and do for life. This contract is entered into through a conversation with your true-self/spiritual-self.

KNOWLEDGE
⇒ 06. 01. 06

When you have knowledge you always know what to do. However, this is not the same as saying when you have knowledge you know everything. The former implies that where you do not know you however know how to ask for help.

LIFE: A MULTIPLE CHOICE TEST
⇒ 16. 01. 06

In a multiple choice test you need to have knowledge to help you decide on the correct answer. Likewise, in life, you need to have knowledge to help you to decide upon appropriate choices that will bring you the results you desire. Hence, life is like a multiple choice test.

LEARNING: A CONTINUOUS PROCESS
⇒ 24. 01. 06

What you know now is what you have learned earlier. At the time of your birth your brain was just like a computer with no software inside. Like a computer that requires to be upgraded time and again, for effectiveness and efficiency, you too must continue to learn to upgrade your brain.

WHAT WE KNOW WE HAVE LEARNED
⇒ 26. 01. 06

In the beginning, i.e. at creation or birth-time, we did not know a thing, and whatever we know is what we have learned from somewhere or someone. Our ancestors had to learn from their experiences all the time. We (modern man) are lucky as we have reference materials to learn from. However, we must continue to learn from both ways. Most importantly, we must always remember that *"what we know we have learned somewhere, to know anything we have to learn something, those who learn something will know something, those who learn something new will know more than what they have always known"*.

EDUCATION: MY DEFINITION
⇒ *30. 01. 06*

An educated individual is one who utilises what he/she has learned (i.e. knowledge and experience), during the learning process (i.e. at the schools, university etc.), to change a life situation from its present state to a better state, relative to the desired results. The general believe that people who come out of the learning process with qualifications are educated is a gross misinterpretation of what education is and should be.

LEARNING
⇒ *30. 01. 06*

It is the first thing that we do after we are born. We learn to communicate, we learn to eat, we learn to move and walk, and we learn to acquire knowledge. Then we know, but we must continue to learn until the end of our time.

EDUCATION/LEARNING/EMPLOYMENT
⇒ 04. 02. 06

Most people believe that we go through the learning process (*i.e. formal*) in order to earn qualifications to find a job. However, the learning process is much more important than it can be just for acquiring qualifications and certificates to find a job. In any case, it is clear now that countries of the world can no longer manage to provide jobs for everyone. Hence, qualifications and certificates can no longer be the major reason for going through the learning process.

Learning should be considered a process of acquiring knowledge in order to manage oneself in life. For that reason, it is very important that all go through the learning curve so they can be well-informed on the basics of managing themselves in life, irrespective of whether they are in employment or not. It is the best thing that can happen to people out of employment, who are prone to frustrations and stress. Knowing how to manage oneself can bring stability in life.

THE BETTER EQUATION IN LIFE
⇒ 09. 02. 06

It is often said that "*what you put your attention to you will get*". Most people in life tend to focus on what they do not have, and the result is usually a feeling of emptiness or nothingness. The habit of always focusing on what you do not have denies people the opportunity to enjoy whatever they may have achieved. This is because as soon as people achieve something they immediately focus on something else they do not have, and the cycle goes on and on until the end of time for such individuals. When you focus on what you do not have, not having is what you will get. Many feel that they have to work hard, make lots of money, then buy things they want, and then become who they want to be and enjoy life. Unfortunately, such an equation never works well. The better equation is to accept who you are now as complete, enjoy what you have, and do what you love, and get the things you want, including money.

OPINIONS GALORE
⇒ 09. 02. 06

There is as many opinions as there are people around the globe. It is less important what people say but more important what people do. What are you doing, as an individual, wherever you are, to make living life an enjoyable experience for you and for others? Opinions on what others are not doing or are doing wrong are less helpful. It is better to take action yourself and do something that will enhance life the way you see things.

MISTAKES
⇒ 09. 02. 06

Mistakes are one of the major factors that have enabled human beings to develop, mentally or psychologically. When you make a mistake, you learn about how not to do something, and you try other options. The result of this becomes experience and knowledge. People who do not make mistakes are those who never do anything.

A MEASURE FOR SUCCESS: MY WISH
⇒ 11. 02. 06

My wish is to influence society to consider success in terms of their purpose for being. Success should be defined in terms of whether or not you have discovered your reason for being or existence on Earth. How much of your purpose are you able to fulfil? Are you living your purpose or not? And how close are you getting to the future you desire i.e. your vision? Your vision is an image of the future you desire based on who you are and what you are here for. A measure for success, therefore, should not be limited to the material world of money and wealth, but instead, the nature and quality of your contributions to life, including how you use your wealth and money.

BETTER MENTAL RICHES AND WEALTH
⇒ 12. 02. 06

It is much better to be mentally rich i.e. with expanded knowledge base, than to be only materially rich. Mental riches can easily be shared whereas there are not many who are willing to part with the so-called "hard-earned" material riches, money inclusive. The sharing of mental riches is easily sustainable, and the receivers can keep forever and improve their lives. Mental riches are less likely to promote greed and competition that could lead to conflicts and deadly wars as do material riches.

OUR MAIN PURPOSE
⇒ 12. 02. 06

We, human beings or the human species, are just one of the many living species on Planet Earth today, and our main purpose should be to promote survival of our own species. Other living species have come and gone before us, such as Dinosaurs etc., and we have come, and we shall also go. In the meantime, "it's our time", and we must use it effectively, to extend our lifetime rather than to shorten it through conflicts and wars.

GIVE WITHOUT EXPECTATIONS
⇒ 17. 02. 06

Mother Nature gives us all that we need to survive for free. Why can't we do the same to help each other to feel complete in life? Let us practice the habit of giving without expectations. Give away love, time, money, food, a helping hand etc.

WORRIES HARDLY MATERIALISE
⇒ 18. 02. 06

It is amazing how we spend most of our lives preoccupied with imaginary worries. Much of what we worry about never becomes a reality. Unfortunately, worries in your mind can give rise to emotional toxins. I have had many experiences of worries that turned out to be non-issues. Once I lived briefly in France and I had this worry of not being able to communicate well in the French language. However, whenever I visited some service points i.e. the Post Office etc., things would always work better than my imaginary worries portrayed.

IDENTITY IN LIFE
⇒ 24. 02. 06

Many people define themselves in terms of what they have i.e. their properties, job positions, qualifications etc. The danger is that when such material things and positions are taken away, for whatever reasons, it creates a feeling of nothingness and hopelessness, and in general life seems meaningless. The other downside is that those without any materials, due to unemployment and other factors, will always feel like they are lesser humans, and hence find it difficult to obtain some level of happiness in life. It is however much better to identify yourself in terms of your purpose for being i.e. the natural reason you believe you were created for. This, nobody can take away, and most importantly focuses on your basic self and what you do to make that needed contribution to life, and hence gives your life meaning.

IT'S OUR TIME
⇒ 03. 03. 06

As the human species, we need to make use of this opportunity, of existence, that God has afforded us, to propel our species to another level of growth up the evolution ladder. Nobody knows for sure how much time has been allocated for the human species, and therefore we need to effectively use what time we have now to celebrate creation rather than be destructive. Some years to come we shall just remain fossils like other species that have come and gone before us. But now is our time. Let us contribute to life and create joy and happiness, which is the desire of most if not all.

LIVING ON PURPOSE
⇒ 03. 03. 06

To be truly happy in life you need to understand the concept of purpose, which will create a sense of meaning and usefulness in your life. You need to fully understand that you were brought into life to make a contribution that will allow for continuity in life, as determined by nature at creation. Every single individual has their own unique purpose that does not depend on attachment to anything or anybody. It is crucial to identify purpose and separate it or detach it from external factors such as the material world. Once purpose has been singled out and detached from external factors it is then possible to continue to live life to the end of your naturally intended time. Even with the loss of external factors, e.g. relationships breaking-up etc., because purpose is your only reason for existence, not the external factors. Loss of the external factors should not make you feel like there is nothing to live for, because you still have your purpose.

WHO WE ARE
⇒ 04. 03. 06

Our foundation in life is at the level of the species where we share a common link to the creator of existence or God. It is at this stage that our purposes in life were installed in us, as a specific human species. Any other differences, be it ethnicity, racial, religious or otherwise, are secondary.

Common among our purposes should be the desire to continue that which creation has afforded us, namely life. We need to each find our purpose through-which all our actions and deeds in life should be determined, rather than the present situation where life is often dominated by activities based on our secondary differences.

OPINIONS
⇒ *04. 03. 06*

You build opinion based upon the knowledge and experience that you have. A difference in opinion usually reflects a difference in the nature of knowledge between the parties involved. As a result, opinions can be a source for new knowledge for people in general. However, you are supposed to use your own opinions to determine the future you desire rather than rely on the opinions of others, which are based on their own desires. Learn from the opinions of others and make your own opinion, and then determine your own future.

IT'S OUR TIME
⇒ *11. 03. 06*

Ample evidence exists from the geological history which indicates that several species have come and gone. There is no doubt that the human species too shall cease to exist at some point in the future, and only leave behind its bodily remains as part of the geological history. Those of us who have existed and are still to exist in the future are certainly the chosen few. It is for this reason therefore that we must celebrate life with happiness and joy in recognition of the opportunity afforded us to live. Judging by our impact on Earth e.g. infrastructure etc., we certainly are not coming from afar, equally, we also seem to be moving at an unsustainably fast rate, perhaps signalling a quick approach to our end time. However, it's our time now, and we need to use it appropriately to support continuity in the life of the human species, with happiness and joy.

CHOOSE PEACE FOR LIFE
⇒ 12. 03. 06

I believe that our highest purpose in life is to promote continuity in life. We do that by working in tandem with the forces of creation, by creating favourable conditions for people to enjoy life and live longer. In order to promote continuity in life we must choose peace at all times. People who choose non-peaceful conditions are working against the forces of creation, and hence are fighting against life itself. However, there is no winning in fighting against life, and usually such people will eventually live miserable lives or will simply get destroyed by the environment they find themselves in. People who associate with those who choose non-peaceful conditions are usually affected in the fight against life, and often also live miserable lives or are eventually destroyed as well. To enjoy life we must choose peace as well as deliberately choose to be with peaceful people at all times.

OPINION
⇒ 19. 03. 06

There is no right or wrong opinion but simply an opinion. Opinion is formed based on knowledge you have. Differences in opinions reflect differences in knowledge. Such differences are a source for knowledge because they indicate that someone may know more or less than you do. To access knowledge from a difference in opinion one must detach from the habit of "the need to be right". Nevertheless, as an individual the ultimate decision on your life choices rests with your own opinion, based on your own knowledge and comprehension of life. Best opinions require an expanded knowledge base.

SPIRIT (YOUR TRUE-SELF) LOVES TO PLAY
⇒ 19. 03. 06

Your spiritual-self, which represents your divine-self, has no sense of age and remains as it was when you were a toddler. Your Spirit loves to play, so give it a break from the ego-determined confinement you keep it in. Go out and play, have fun and take care, it is the best way to promote your wellness. Break those ego-created barriers that keep your Spirit in solitary confinement i.e. the do's and don'ts that we impose on ourselves either because of peer-pressure or societal pressure. Like when you suddenly shy away from the activities you enjoy simply because people think you are old to continue, even though your Spirit is dying to continue. Remember that when Spirit is happy, you have total wellness in your life. If you bottle-up your Spirit there is a huge potential that in no time you will explode, and when that happens your relationships greatly suffer. So, go on and let your Spirit loose, unlike the ego element Spirit has no bad intentions, and hence you do not have to worry about any bad consequences. But first things first, learn to distinguish between your ego-self and your spiritual-self (divine-self), and then listen to the voice of your Spirit and "just do it" as the people at Nike like to say.

OPENING-UP TO KNOWLEDGE
$\Rightarrow$ 24. 03. 06

Opening-up to knowledge means accepting all new knowledge without question, and then you make your own follow-up enquiry or little research to find out more on the subject. It is an advantage, in many ways, to open-up to knowledge:

◊ Even if you do not agree or understand now, you may grow to like the idea later.

◊ You may find that other people benefit from discussing the idea at a later date, and hence you would be making a difference, even if you don't agree or like the idea yourself.

◊ Acquiring knowledge expands your knowledge base and upgrades your brain thought-mechanism that generates purposeful ideas.

◊ Opening-up to new knowledge develops the

habit of "valuing the difference" in cases of differences of opinion.
◊ Similarly, opening-up to new knowledge transforms the habit of "the need to be right".

So, open-up to knowledge and become an effective being.

LIFE ON EXPECTATIONS
⇒ 19. 04. 06

It is preferable to live a life without expectations from the external world, since we do not have any control of such. However, many people have chosen to live a life of expectations and yet have not learned how to deal with unfulfilled expectations. What you have to understand is that:
◊ Living a life of expectations is a choice you make
◊ Living a life of expectations require that you learn how to manage yourself to deal with unfulfilled expectations
◊ There is only one person you can control; that is yourself.

WHAT WE KNOW WE HAVE LEARNED
⇒ 19. 04. 06

The difference between us is not in our being, but rather, in our doing. We all are born as human beings, with inborn purposes that determine our being. However, what we do is determined by what we know, and so is how we live our lives. Learning is the process that will provide us with knowledge. Knowledge is what we use to decide upon our life's choices of whether to do one thing or the other.

LIFE: A CAUSE FOR HAPPINESS
⇒ 20. 04. 06

Many people who spend their lives searching for happiness, and frustrated most of the times, have not accepted that the opportunity to exist in life is the biggest gift ever. Such people have, instead of giving back something, turned their back on their creator, and are looking elsewhere for something they believe will be better than life. It is hard to think of anything that could be larger than life.

LEARNING: THE ONLY DOOR TO EDUCATION
⇒ 01. 05. 06

It is very important to note that anyone who wishes to live a meaningful and enjoyable life must anchor their personal development on the foundation of learning. This is because learning is the only lead to becoming a knowledgeable and educated person, with a potential to discover your reason for being. However, it is also important to be aware that although learning is the only door to education, it does not guarantee such. This is because learning entails the process of acquiring new knowledge to expand your brain capacity and knowledge base.

Education on the other hand includes the process of tapping into your knowledge base, through your brain thought-mechanism, to initiate and effect changes in life, from the status quo to a desired level. The world today is however inhabited by a great many people who are learned but have not reached the level of being educated, because most discontinued the learning process on the attainment of certificates of learning. The learning process, at the learning institutes, is an exercise designed to teach us how to learn so that we can then continue on our own throughout life. The certificates that we receive are a testimony to the fact that we have the potential to learn. These certificates are usually given at the end of a learning period based on individual's assessment, through examinations or tests, on their ability to recall what they have learnt. In other words, these certificates are not education certificates but they are effectively learning certificates. Unfortunately, many consider them to be education certificates and then they stop learning, believing that they are educated. Consequently, such individuals will experience a lack of brain development and stagnation of knowledge base, leading to complete ineffectiveness in the management of self in life.

THE NEED TO BE RIGHT
⇒ *01. 05. 06*

There is yet no evidence to indicate that anyone is born already with knowledge inside of them. In the absence of such evidence, we can assume that everything that we know we have learnt. Equally, there is more we do not know yet. Amazingly, some people can be so stuck to their ego-driven "need to be right" to the extent of fuelling conflicts, some of which are life-threatening and even deadly.

INFLUENCE HAPPINESS: STOP BLAME
⇒ *04. 05. 06*

It is preferable to share our differing opinions rather than blame others for being different from us, in opinion and deeds. When you share your opinions you actually share knowledge that can help improve the effectiveness of others. When, on the other hand, you blame you make others feel different and less human, and they automatically become subjected to emotional toxins. To a large extent, our daily stimuli determines how the day shall progress, such that blame can trigger negative emotions that will adversely affect all our daily relationships. The result is that more people will end up unhappy as compared to the one person originally affected.

OPINION: DIFFERENT VIEWS
⇒ *04. 05. 06*

The fact that one differs or sees differently from others is an indication of the disparity in the level of knowledge and experience (practical knowledge). There is absolutely no need to start a conflict, rather, determine the difference and bridge the gap through learning. Most importantly, abandon "the need to be right".

LEARNING FOR OPPORTUNITIES OR SELF MANAGEMENT?
⇒ 05. 05. 06

For decades most people believed that we attend the school learning system in order to attain qualifications to find a better job. If this has been the case it now has become history as evidenced by the multitudes of many learned individuals, with the right qualifications, but cannot find jobs. The real reason though, I believe, for going through the school system, is to learn how to learn and then continue to learn all life, in order to sustain effective self-management in life. This is even more relevant now given more and more people find themselves out of employment, and hence need to develop skills for effective self-management in life.

HUMAN EFFECTIVENESS AND EFFICIENCY
⇒ 07. 05. 06

It is preferable to focus on the present and lookout to the future than the past. Focusing on the past encourages and nurtures the habit of procrastination, due to the resultant worries about what could have been or not have been. Ultimately, operating from the past leads to a state of insanity as one tries to be in the present but lives in the past. You must spend more time on determining the solutions to your problems than on endlessly analyzing the problems. Problems are undesirable occurrences (faults) that lead to undesirable experiences and results (effects). Hence, you want to spend more time on determining how you can stop them from recurring, in order to avoid experiencing the non-desirable effects. By focusing on the cause, and changing it, you have a better chance to achieve the desired results or experiences i.e. effects.

THE FUTURE YOU DESIRE
⇒ 07. 05. 06

To create the results you desire in your life, you need to undertake the following simple procedures:

◊ Determine, first, what you desire
◊ Learn how to create the results you desire
◊ Then do, to create the results you desire

The three steps are a must, otherwise there is never going to be that future you desire. The only other alternative is the adage "*if you do not know where you are going any road will lead you there*". It doesn't matter whether you complain and blame the government for the weather, the three steps above are a pre-requisite for the future you desire. Ultimately, everyone is responsible for their own deeds and life on Earth, and there is no blaming others for your destiny.

MAKING A LIVING
⇒ 12. 05. 06

In making a living you must remember that no matter how much you make, nothing you make shall ever surpass the gift of life you receive from your creator. It is preferable to spend the gift of life sharing it with others, as a thank you gesture to the one who created you. When you go to work, wherever you work, consider it as giving away your time, knowledge and ability etc., to others as a contribution to life. When those you serve appreciate and thank you for your service, rejoice as that would be a sign that your purpose in life is being fulfilled. Need you look for any other meaning in your life? Not at all!

A WISH FOR THE HUMAN SPECIES
⇒ 13. 05. 06

I would love for people to see life as a precious and joyous gift they wouldn't trade for anything else. It would be preferable and inspirational, especially to the young, if people would change their vocabulary of defining life like it was an unpleasant experience e.g. sweat and toil, struggle, survival of the fittest, dog eat dog, a jungle out there etc. Such expressions create a negative feeling in others and portrays life as a non-enjoyable experience, and ultimately most feel life has no meaning, is dull and not worth living.

PURPOSE: THE NATURAL MOTIVATOR
⇒ 13. 05. 06

There is absolutely no reason why we could have been created for nothing; purposeful living is what we were created for. People who have purpose in life live happy and fulfilling lives. It is people who do not have or have not discovered their purpose for being who find life meaningless and non-enjoyable.

Purpose is one element that can succeed in toppling money and wealth as the focus of most people's goals. When you have purpose you are self-motivated to provide first-class service, with no complaints or blames. If money and wealth were to be suddenly phased-out the majority of people would not turn-up for work, because they would not have any other reason to do so. However, purposeful people would continue to serve.

PERRSONAL EFFECTIVENESS
⇒ 14. 05. 06

Learn from others, but create your own destiny. No one can tell you how to enjoy your life but only you know what brings joy to you. You can create that which brings joy to you by learning from others, who may have gone a similar route in the past.

HUMAN LIFE EXPERIENCE
⇒ 15. 05. 06

In geology there is a saying that "the best geologist is the one who has seen all the rocks". This can equally be applied to motivate human life experience through the expression "the best human being is the one who has experienced all forms of life's environments". In life one has to experience different ways of living in order to fully appreciate the essence of the life experience.

Whereas most people would feel disadvantaged, and even cursed, to find themselves living in what could be termed low-class areas, such as in villages or townships, I personally have fond memories of my days as a toddler and youngster living in such conditions. Today I have been to some of the big cities of the world, e.g. London and Paris, but I still cherish memories of my life in the townships and lands, where I grew up. Most importantly, I feel that my life is truly a journey across all life's experiences, and it gives me great pleasure.

WEALTH: MY VIEW
⇒ 17. 05. 06

The value of life can not be measured in terms of wealth. As individuals we do not need to accumulate wealth in order to survive, rather, we need to help others to survive by creating jobs and providing service. The accumulation of large quantities of wealth by individuals, for themselves, can only serve to demoralize others as they feel not having is equivalent to meaningless life. Wealth often leads to greed, and with that comes conflict and crime. However, the basic form of life consists of service, to produce necessities to meet the basic needs of all, at no price at all.

WHAT YOU FOCUS ON YOU GET
⇒ 25. 05. 06

You will always get what you focus on. Many of you often focus on not having a good life, money, this and that etc. The general feeling you have in life is that of having nothing all the time, and hence, a meaningless life. Even if you do achieve whatever you wanted your mind immediately shifts to something else you want. The result is that you live the rest of your life non-appreciative of what you already have, with a feeling of emptiness and meaningless life. Make a change and focus on what you have now and enjoy it, and do the things you love to do in order to experience the joy of a meaningful life. Remember the saying "yesterday is history, tomorrow the future, but today is the present", meaning present as in "gift", so enjoy the gift now.

HUMAN EFFECTIVENESS IN SERVICE
⇒ 25. 05. 06

Many people end up in most jobs simply because they have their focus on getting that which they want, rather than for a course to serve life. This is again a case of focusing on making money to get things. I however believe there is more joy in working not for money, but rather, for the sake of service itself. Realising that the service we provide makes a larger impact in improving the lives of many people should be the real essence of work. This allows everyone to share their natural gifts through service to generate meaning and joy in the lives of others. By offering our gifts through service we allow for the provision of infrastructure i.e. roads, hospitals etc., and basic needs such as food and shelter, through farming and the construction of houses. Any member of the human species who aspires to attain a level of effectiveness, and develop further, must adopt the approach of work for service rather than work for getting and having (things).

IT'S OUR TIME
⇒ *31. 05. 06*

The Geological Timescale indicates that different life-forms have had their own time-slots on Planet Earth, since the beginning of life. The human species too has its own time-slot that began at the creation of the first human beings. Within the entire slot for the human species every individual has his/her own slot, during which he/she shall live to experience the life process on Planet Earth. Now, it is up to you to use your time effectively.

PROBLEMS
⇒ 17. 06. 06

These are experiences of undesirable outcomes, and everyone goes through them. Problems indicate that something is not as expected and require to be acted upon. Problems should not be a cause for concern but rather a cause for action to create the preferred or desired experiences. Concern alone would magnify the undesired experience and make it overwhelming.

THE POWER OF CHOICE
⇒ 17. 06. 06

Everyone has inside of them the natural power to choose anything they prefer in life. Despite the believe by most people that life is money, such that most are unable to enjoy life because of their focus on the illusive element of money, it is possible through "the power of choice", to change focus and aim at other aspects (natural) of life. For example, it is practical to change focus from the element of money centred relationships to other forms of relationships like these:

◊ *Time*-centred relationships, where you give away your time to others, and your most empowering lead questions are of the form "How can I best spend my time today?"

◊ *Knowledge*-centred relationships, where you share your experiences and knowledge with others, and your most empowering lead questions are of the form "What knowledge can I share today?", which could save lives!!.

◊ *Service*-centred relationships, where you offer your service to others through various forums, including your employment, as a way of contributing to life. In this case your most empowering lead questions are of the form "How can I raise my work contribution and effectiveness in order to assist my customers?"

THE BEST OF LIFE: RELATIONSHIPS
⇒ 23. 06. 06

As the saying goes "the best things in life are free", nothing could be truer than this with regard to our relationships with others.

The best relationships are the free, natural ones, based on the desire to relate, rather than those based on need. Needs demand to be met, and failure leads to frustrations.

THE OLDER THE WISER
⇒ 28. 06. 06

It is often said that the older you get the wiser you become, this in recognition of the wisdom of elderly persons, emanating from a wealth of knowledge and experience, amassed over the years. If you continue to grow old but still find it difficult to express joy in life, it can only be explained in the saying "growing old rather than growing whole". People who have been around (*in life*) should at some point master the art of living fulfilling lives.

Unfortunately, the world is full of people who struggle by day, and hardly experience the joy of life. The biggest hurdle, it seems, is the love for monetary wealth and the material world, which are hard to come by for the majority of the world population, yet these are not specifically basic needs in themselves. As the wise usually say "if you keep on doing things the same way you will always get the same results", perhaps it is time for people to change from focusing on the material world and try something else.

THE POWER OF PURPOSE
⇒ 29. 06. 06

Purpose allows individuals to feel fulfilled in their lives. Once uncovered one can easily determine the life relationships they desire to associate with i.e. sports, politics, religion, education etc. Such relationships allow one to live their purpose with passion, and to experience joy in life. Such is the power of purpose.

IT'S OUR TIME, YOUR TIME TOO!
⇒ 29. 06. 06

At times people go through difficulties in life and begin to experience despair and hopelessness. For any such people, here is my word of encouragement:: "Somewhere around the globe, your country, your community, and your workplace, there is a little spot at which you will find real people like you. These people really love you, and enjoy the same things you like, and would like to share their experience of joy with you. All you have to do is to get out of the little hole you live in and find these people, and experience the ultimate joy in life. If you choose to remain holed-in, it would be difficult for the people that loves and cares about you to find you, and it would be impossible for you to access the relationships you desire to experience in life. So, crawl out of there!"

Human beings are a unique species in that we have the ability to imagine, and experience what others go through, and be able to encourage, offer support, and share in the joys of life. Unfortunately, we have not been able to master this uniquely humane way of living, and worst still, we have failed to impress upon our young to appreciate it. As a result many people would rather live their lives holed-in, oblivious of the fact that out there, "there is help for them too".

The tragedy of such a missing link is people, especially the young, unable to cope and manage themselves well in life, eventually giving-up on life prematurely.

THE POWER OF PURPOSE
⇒ *01. 07. 06*

When you are on purpose, it almost does not matter whether or not you will reach your vision. What matters is that you are following the right direction to where you desire to go, and all your daily activities are purposeful, and hence fulfil your reason for being. Along the route to your vision, you will experience joy, as you engage in the different activities that you come upon. The very fact that you are engaged in activities that fulfil your purpose, and gives you joy, is enough to create meaning in your life; it is the essence of living.

TRUE HAPPINESS
⇒ *04. 07. 06*

Many people believe that working hard to earn a living is what shall bring about happiness in their lives. The truth though is that only through continuous, life-long learning, can one know and master how to create a lasting state of happiness for themselves, and others, in life. No amount of material riches or gains can bring about lasting happiness, and even so, there just cannot be enough job positions to afford everyone any great amount of wealth. The reality is that the majority of the world population shall continue, throughout their entire lives, without having attained any amount of the material riches, despite the day to day struggle to have such. The solution lies in knowledge, to manage oneself and decide upon desirable and life enhancing choices.

LIFE: A MULTIPLE CHOICE TEST
⇒ 12. 07. 06

In life, one can choose between a simply prepared chicken meal, with just salt and water, and a multi-spiced chicken meal as that you may find in any Indian restaurant. Eating is a natural practice driven by the bodies need for essential elements, for its nourishment and effective function, and keeping alive. However, our choices of what food we eat is largely influenced by the taste we enjoy rather than the quality of food, with regard to the needed essentials. As a result, although chicken cooked the simple way (salt and water) has relatively the same quantity in basic essentials as that spiced-up, most people would prefer the latter because of its enhanced taste.

Similarly, life could be lived in a simple and less complicated way, but the majority of people prefer the spiced option.

The reality is that today's life is at the mercy of wealth/money, such that the more spices one desires the more money they should have or make. Unfortunately, most people will never enjoy life due to the preference of spices and the elusiveness of the element of money.

THE EVOLVING BEHAVIOUR
⇒ 08. 09. 06

The human brain has developed to allow us to distinguish between behaviours that promote desirable and non-desirable results, in terms of living life. How then is it that some of us still require to be controlled, like non-human animals considered to have less developed brains? If you are any of those that behave badly ask yourself these empowering questions, to improve your behaviour:

◊ Who am I and why do I behave in an undesirable manner?
◊ What is the future I desire from my behaviours?

THE FUTURE YOU DESIRE
⇒ 24. 09. 06

To create or reach the future you desire you need to put your attention on the activities of your mission. These are the do's you should accomplish to get you from the present to nearer your vision. It is important to focus on what you can do rather than what you cannot, in order to get your mission wheels rolling toward the future you desire. Most people spend too much time focusing on why they cannot do A or B, unfortunately, this cannot get the mission rolling towards the future desired. The wise often say "what you put your attention to you shall get", hence, if you too focus on what you cannot do, what you cannot do is what will always prevail in your life.

LIFE: BIGGER THAN ANY
28. 09. 06

Life is the biggest gift ever, and hence it is proper to live everyday celebrating this aspect. For those who are still searching and asking for something better to ignite happiness in their lives, they might as well realise that theirs is an infinite search. The gift of life is all we ever needed. Anything else is meant to support life and can never surpass life as the most sought-after item in the world of existence. Picture this, you could be the richest there ever has been but if your life is taken then you are no more. On the contrary, if only your riches are taken away you still have your life and purpose to continue living like all other living species. Therefore, life has nothing to do with the material world, instead the material world has all to do with life.

WORTHINESS REFLECTS PURPOSE
⇒ 01. 10. 06

Everyone likes to feel that they are important and worthy beings. This usually shows up in the form of activities that people do to contribute in life. The contribution makes people feel worthy and therefore needed in life. Once that realisation happens, individuals begin to sense a feeling of meaning in their lives, which reflects a sign of purposefulness. People who never do anything, and are always asking from others, can never experience a feeling of usefulness, and will never find meaning in their lives. Such people have no sense of worth and their lives have no purpose, until they begin to share something with others. Ultimately, our worthiness is a reflection of our purpose for being.

THE POWER OF KNOWLEDGE
$\Rightarrow$ 06. 10. 06

Everything that you do, in every other minute of your life, follows a decision you make (aware or unaware). The choices you make are reached after making a decision; the decisions range from split-second decisions to long-term decisions. To decide, you use knowledge and nothing else. The act of decision making is a response to stimuli, which is in the form of an inquiry e.g. a question. You then consult your knowledge bank, make an interpretation, and then respond by making a choice; that is the process of decision-making.

KNOWLEDGE: SAD REALITY
$\Rightarrow$ 07. 10. 06

As the wise have observed, "you can take a horse for drinking but you can not force it to drink". Likewise, you can offer people knowledge but you can not force them to use it. People prefer to exercise their right to choice, and hence, whether or not they will use knowledge offered depends on them exercising that right.

KNOW WHO YOU ARE AND WHY YOU ARE HERE
⇒ 17. 10. 06

Unless you know who you are, and what you came into this world to do, you will never feel fulfilled in life. Many people think that who they are is what they have e.g. a work position, material property etc., however, many still who have achieved such remain unfulfilled, and continue to view life as a struggle. This is because not knowing who you are and what brings you here results in doing what everyone else is doing, which may have nothing to do with your inner-self desires. Hence, you will always experience an everlasting inner-feeling of being unfulfilled, until the end of time.

The aspect of the ego controls and drives you to always compete and excel to beat all others, and become better than everyone else. However, there is never a time to experience complete fulfilment and total joy in life. The moment you get one thing you immediately sense a lack in other aspects, and so on and so on, till the end of your time.

To enjoy life and feel fulfilled, know who you are and what you are here for.

THROUGH THE EYES OF "THE EVOLVING SPECIES"
⇒ 24. 10. 06

Through my eyes I only see one *Homo sapiens*. Any other factions of the human species are secondary, and are only meant to establish order and effective management of the process of living. Such organisational factions are nature's strategic management systems. Organisational factions allow for diversity in life, and hence create a variety of events that give life sparkling beauties. Imagine if we had exactly the same activities all across the globe. Chances are we would never find joy in exploring the world, and hence we would not travel anywhere. Life would be uneventful and much of a bore, and we would probably live shorter life spans.

DEATH: LESSON FOR WELLNESS
⇒ 25. 10. 06

No doubt we are aware of the fact that nobody can stop death. Equally, most are aware that death can be caused by negligence on our part as humans. Many deaths are caused by deteriorating health status which may be related to a variety of reasons, largely of socio-economic aspects. Many of such reasons can be explicitly defined and hence mitigated against. An unfortunate reality is that most people remain non-proactive in matters of their own health until illness or death strikes. When death arrives we are often engulfed in grief and sorrow, and then we simply say "well, it's life, what can we do?" However, I believe that each death provides a lesson that can help those still in life to improve their wellness. There are several empowering questions that one could ask, such as:

- ◊ What can I learn from this death?
- ◊ What really happened?
- ◊ How can I avoid what happened?
- ◊ Who can I ask for help?

This way death becomes a real lesson to improve the lives of the living.

LIFE IS AS IS: FIND YOUR OWN NICHE
⇒ 26. 10. 06

I truly believe that you cannot fight against life and win. Life as you see it is in its natural form, and hence, for you to survive you must find your own niche that will be supportive and favourable. Many people try to change life to suit their wishes and desires but unfortunately many such people end up in despair, and may give up on life. There is just no way to change life, as it represents nature's way, but we can change ourselves to fit into life. Take the example of zebras in the Chobe National Park, where they are constantly tormented by the lords of the jungles i.e. lions. Lions have got silky hunting skills that make the Zebra easy-meat when in the jungle. In the Chobe National Park however zebras prefer to graze in the open plains, which allow them ample security from the lions as it is much easier to spot the fierce predators at a distance, and be attentive to avoid being caught.

The lesson here is that the Zebra did not opt for fighting against the Lion in the jungle but instead found its own niche where its survival is better secured. If you go to the Chobe National Park you will often spot herds of zebras "alive and kicking", enjoying themselves without fear. The Lion, out of frustration, sometimes is forced to chase directly without employing his silky hiding skills, but the Zebra on the other hand, within the open plains, has room enough to pack a real shot in doubles, and kicks real hard. Similarly, as humans we must learn to find our own niche in life, where we can live happily with joy despite life's adversities. Our greatest kick is in the use of knowledge, to manage ourselves and to create the future we desire.

LIFE CONTINUES
⇒ 27. 10. 06

It is said that "even after we are gone life goes on". Hence, it is upon individuals to put their lives in their own hands. Take initiatives to improve your own health, and equally, aim to attain some level of personal growth to help you create total wellness. Do not put your life in the hands of others, thinking that maybe life depends on your existence, and hence everyone will want to help you. The reality is that even after you are gone people will continue to live in your absence, and you shall be forgotten by most unless if you leave a profound legacy. Now is the time to live your own human experience, and therefore, take care of yourself. Ultimately, life continues like you have never been here.

YOUR WORTH
⇒ 27. 10. 06

Your usefulness is what will determine meaningfulness in your life. How useful you are depends on that which you do which others will find helpful. It is about contributing something useful or helpful rather than wanting things. Realise that focusing on wanting things can never make you a useful and worthy being.

LIVING LIFE OR WAITING FOR DEATH
⇒ 29. 10. 06

Many people struggle in life because they prefer to work for the material world rather than for the natural course of promoting life. If you choose not to work because you are not paid then you will spend your life doing nothing. In other words, through your birth, you were brought into life and then all you did was sit and wait until death caught up with you. This is simply waiting for death. There are many things that anyone can choose to do to express their living life. The highest purpose in life should be about making a contribution, as an individual, and thereby signalling your presence and active role in the process of living life. Rather than just sleep and get up, and sleep again and get up again, you could give a hand to others in many various ways that would define your usefulness in life, and hence meaning in your life. The million dollar question now is "whether you want to live and participate in life or you simply want to wait for death while you watch others living?."

LIFE
⇒ 07. 11. 06

Life is the relationships that we have on Planet Earth. The relationships with each other, with other species we depend on, and with nature in general. Life is not the material world that most struggle so much to have, rather, we need the material world to support our relationships. The high point of life is the joyous experiences we obtain from our relationships.

A MISSING LINK IN LIFE
⇒ 10. 11. 06

My most empowering affirmation says "what we know we have learned and what we do not know we must learn". Subsequently, I believe that life should be the biggest subject that we need to learn about. However, this does not seem to be the case, instead many of us live by "trial and error". For everyone to afford the joy of life, it is imperative that we first learn how to manage ourselves in life. The concept of management of self in life is what remains a major missing link in human life.

SOCIETY INEFFECTIVENESS
⇒ 19. 11. 06

In today's society everyone is an advisor but none gets to turn the advice into practice. In other words, most people are not proactively responsive to advice and knowledge, and instead they have chosen to expect from others other than themselves. People advise and expect their advice to be turned into reality by someone else, and when such does not happen they complain, blame, criticize, condemn, and castigate. Such is the order of life in today's society.

Our purpose however can never be to expect from others but to take part in creating the future we all desire, by turning our own ideas into reality through being proactive. Rather than complain, choose to share your opinions and experiences. Rather than blame, criticize, condemn and castigate, choose to teach, guide, coach and encourage. Rather than conflict, choose peace.

GOD: THE CREATOR
⇒ 08. 12. 06

God the Creator loves all equally and does not condemn, criticize, blame, hate, abuse, discriminate, control, or punish. God does not make choices for us on how to live life but supports those who support life. God does not see different people but only living beings. God is the creator of all forms of existence, and us humans are only a small part of that existence. God is the creator as well as the provider, and as humans we have our variable ways through which we show gratitude.

The human species, and other species, as well as all forms of matter and the basic elements of existence, are the products of God the Creator, and he loves all his creations. However you comprehend God the Creator is fine, as long as it helps bring meaning, happiness, and joy in your life, and does not put the lives of others in danger. Always remember that the creator of existence "loves and supports" all his creations, and hence, life supports those who supports it. Blame, criticism, condemnation, discrimination, abuse, judgement, misbehaviour, lawlessness etc. etc., are not supportive to life, and hence life will not support those who indulge in such.

God the creator of existence has given us tools we need to survive and enjoy the life experiences. One such powerful tool is the brain system, whose thought-mechanism helps us to determine our preferred choices to live life. Now, we can use the brain to realize "the power of knowledge" and use it to discover "the power of purpose", and ultimately comprehend "the power of choice", and then select only life-supportive acts of living.

COMPLAINTS ABOUT LIFE
⇒ 21. 01. 07

I consider myself a natural living species, much like a plant species in the middle of some land, or fish species in the middle of some ocean. Nature supports us all equally, albeit in different ways, wherever we exist. I have accepted my life as it is, and continue to live it in a way that I prefer. My contributions are ways through-which I thank my creator for giving me the opportunity to experience this wonderful process of life.

Now, my view concerning people who complain about life is that such people have not yet accepted the gift of life, given to them by their creator. Hence, living life is not something that such people appreciate and enjoy. In general, every individual lives their life based on their own preferred choices, hence any complaints about life are misguided. Unfortunately, many people have a tendency to evade responsibility of their own lives, and instead resort to blaming others for failing to obtain meaning and happiness in their lives.

NO HEALTH: NO FUTURE
⇒ 21. 01. 07

It is imperative that all people become aware that there is no future to build and enjoy if they neglect their health. First things in the life of every individual should necessarily include health. The neglect of health implies:

- ◊ No future to build
- ◊ No relationships to enjoy
- ◊ No vacation to enjoy
- ◊ No money to make
- ◊ No thing to do or have.

Let first things first mean your health first.

GOD'S HORROR
⇒ 24. 01. 07

God must be horrified at the sight that is human beings of today. Having provided us with all that we need to live and enjoy the life experience e.g. the brain (natural computer), with its thought mechanism that generate ideas, it is amazing how humanity chose to live a life of struggles. Much like the computer that is used in every workplace, often loaded with a variety of software and capable of a plethora of applications but only utilized for a few, the human brain is hugely under-utilized. With such a mighty organ, we need not be experiencing so much hardship as is often the case the world over. Surely, God must watch in disbelief.

STUDENTS TEACHERS
⇒ 28. 01. 07

It is important that we be teachers as well as students, always. Often times we tend to be all advisors, with very few or none receiving the advice, let alone using it.

LIFE FOR THE INDIVIDUAL
⇒ 05. 02. 07

Determine first how you want to live your life, based on who you are and what you believe you came into life to do i.e. your purpose for being. In other words, or in familiar language, ask yourself this: "what is it you want to do to make a positive difference in life?"

LIFE IS AS IS
⇒ 21. 02. 07

Human beings were created and introduced into life in much the same way that all other species were i.e. both *flora* and *fauna*. What we do in life or the way we live our lives on Earth is a manifestation of our own choices. While other species have to a great extent maintained a natural way of living, we humans have instead greatly spiced-up our living process. The latest example includes the introduction of technology into human life. Many of the man-made additions into the way of life, by humans, have come with both advantages and disadvantages. The worst of such life spices include wealth, which has generated greed and ultimately bloody conflicts. There is also a negative impact on the shared environment, caused by man-made products. Nevertheless, there is no evidence to suggest that the human population could have gone extinct in the event we followed a more natural way of living, like other species. Today many people live their lives in distress and frustrations, due to failure to cope with the present set-up of human life. My advice to people in general is that they need not feel pressured, but instead, just understand that the life habits prevailing today are just the human choice, which every individual can change or modify to suit their own preferences. What we do every day is just one way we have decided, as humans, to spend life, as a way of expressing living life.

Not being able to excel in one thing or the other should not seem like a matter of life and death. Our activities should be seen as a way of expressing our living life, including the necessary contributions we need to sustain life. Such activities should not be used to consider some people better than others, which can demoralise sections of the human species, as they begin to feel less human than others.

The most important thing is to have a purpose to live for, through-which one can determine ways they can contribute to life. Everyone can have a purpose, which allows them to contribute in their preferred ways, and hence minimize frustrations and distress, due to failure in some other activities.

LIFE FOR THE HUMAN SPECIES
⇒ 26. 02. 07

What we do as human beings is not a matter of life and death. What we do is what we choose to do because we believe it will enhance our life experience. Therefore, people should not be afraid to fail because failing is a learning point. Most importantly, everyone should strive to contribute something, no matter how small, because your contribution is what signals your effectiveness, and worth, as a human being.

Everyone was born for a purpose, and they fulfil that purpose by making meaningful contribution to life, through a variety of roles in life. I urge all people living, in their various roles, to always strive for some additional improvement in what they do, as this would result in their personal growth. Ultimately, humans the world over, will attain growth in the level of their effectiveness in terms of living life.

My priority wish is that people begin to work for the success of contribution rather than material gains. The former is an opportunity for the prolongation of human life and a chance to eradicate conflicts.

SERVICE: A LIFE-SUPPORT SYSTEM
⇒ 20. 03. 07

Many will agree that service is a necessary life-support system without which life would be such an unbearable experience. However, most would comprehend the life-support aspect from the point of view of work for a salary or some other rewards for their personal being. I believe though that there is a higher aspect through-which humans should view service as a life-support system. My comprehension of life allows me a view that portrays service as a natural-necessity, which we all need to undertake, not for our personal being but for the entire process of life.

Life requires that we do in order to create that which we need to grow, to survive, to thrive, and to prolong our reign on Planet Earth. This is more than just serving to put food on the table, as is the general consensus, when service is viewed at the scale of a job. Service is what we need to build the schools for our personal growth, the communication facilities to improve our interactions and enjoy our human relations etc. etc. Imagine what would happen if overnight there emerges a new world order to the effect that the element of money is discontinued. Many people would immediately stop going to work, because they understand "work for pay" rather than "work for life service", and there would be dire consequences.

A SIGN OF EVOLUTION
⇒ 22. 03. 07

Human beings belong to the kingdom of animals as compared to the kingdom of plants. In fact many of us do show, to a variable extent, several basic animal instincts e.g. fight or flight. However, humans represent a step in evolution from the basic level of being simply animals to another specific form i.e. the human form. The human form when compared with other animals is marked by an advanced brain that allows, in addition to fight or flight, several other remarkable traits such as reasoning, imagination, envisioning, and choice.

WELLNESS
$\Rightarrow$ 13. 04. 07

Many people lack responsiveness to knowledge in general, including that about their own wellness. Usually, health matters are relegated to lower priorities in preference for things i.e. the material world. Individuals almost leave their entire health to the care of doctors or other health practitioners. The result is that many of the current ailments, which could be easily prevented, tend to go out of control, and ultimately leading to unnecessary sufferings as well as loss of life.

Many people when advised on health matters pretend they have all under control or will simply make excuses such as "I have been living like this for a long time and there is no problem". Many however continue to die and only the immediate cause of death is noted, and many still in life have no idea that often the cause of death is the sum of past non-healthy living habits.

Our life styles i.e. eating habits, social life, health care etc., all have a role in determining our total wellness and how long we shall live. The process of health deterioration is cumulative and ultimately the body cannot cope anymore. The reality is that although we may seem pretty well each morning we do not have an idea how much time is left before the body is made dysfunctional. Depending on our varied life styles our bodies too will deteriorate at varied rates, and eventually become dysfunctional at different times. Through health consciousness, and responsiveness to knowledge on preventative initiatives, we can indeed minimise the rate of deterioration of our bodies and help prolong its life.

THE EFFECTIVE TEACHER
$\Rightarrow$ 13. 04. 07

The effective teacher does not condemn, criticize or blame. Our effectiveness in life is strongly based on learning to develop our brain thought-mechanism. Learning however requires the guidance of an effective teacher.

To effectively teach and influence learners, in a positive way, the teacher must refrain from condemnation, criticism, or blame. Condemnation, criticism or blame only serves to portray the learner as being less-human than the teacher, and hence, acts as a block to learning.

TO ENJOY LIFE
⇒ 18. 07. 07

If you want to enjoy your life start first by focusing on yourself. Develop yourself i.e. personal growth, through the learning process. Learn skills of how to manage yourself in life. Equally, learn how to relate with others in an effective way. Most importantly, you must love yourself and then love others.

EFFECTIVE LIVING
⇒ 18. 07. 07

It is said that the best way to live life is to use all our internal personal natural resources i.e. resourceful ideas, physical energy etc., so that by the time we die we feel totally used up and exhausted (i.e. spent), and all that remains is just waste to through away.

Many people however have and still die with all their beautiful ideas confined inside of them, as well as enormous internal energy resources, never used and going to waste.

Ask yourself this now: "What resourceful ideas do I have in my mind that I could turn into reality, and make some meaningful contribution into life?" Discuss with others and seek assistance from those supportive. It is the only way to manage yourself effectively and end up using your internal resources while still in life.

YOUR SPIRITUAL-SELF: SELF AWARENESS
⇒ 27. 08. 07

Your spiritual-self is your link to your source through-which you can access the same power that created you, and use it to create the future you desire. It is important to develop self-awareness at all times because this is the only way to recognise your spiritual-self, as well as manifestations of your wishes, desires and prayers. Self-awareness will allow you to separate your thoughts, ideas, opinions and desires on the basis of your spiritual-self/inner-self/true-self and the ego-self/conditional-self, and ultimately choose wisely to attain effective living.

VISION: YOUR LIVE LINE
⇒ 05. 09. 07

In an electric power grid when the transmission lines are cut the line is not live anymore, it becomes dead. Similarly, when you have no vision the power of creation, from your source, is not utilised because there is nothing you desire to create. Hence, you seem like a dead power line.

THE BEN MODIE VISION

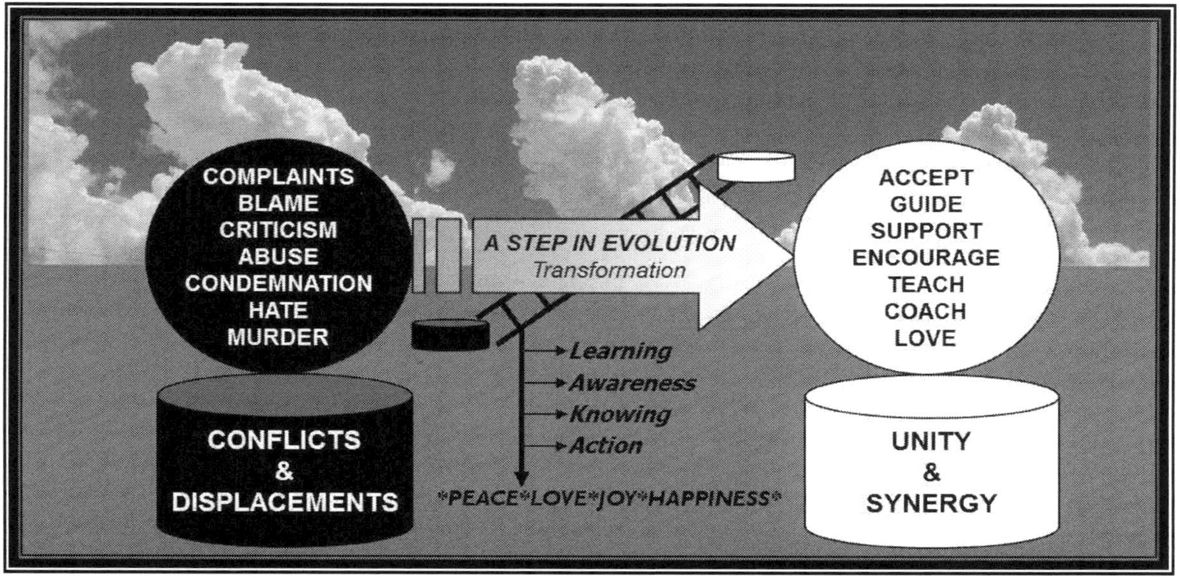
COMPLAINTS
BLAME
CRITICISM
ABUSE
CONDEMNATION
HATE
MURDER
CONFLICTS
&
DISPLACEMENTS
A STEP IN EVOLUTION
Transformation
Learning
Awareness
Knowing
Action
*PEACE*LOVE*JOY*HAPPINESS*
ACCEPT
GUIDE
SUPPORT
ENCOURAGE
TEACH
COACH
LOVE
UNITY
&
SYNERGY

CfK Books

GET YOUR OWN COPY NOW!

For **BOTSWANA** customers please call:

71624001 /

74135747

---

1. THE WISDOM OF THE EVOLVING SPECIES
Inspired words to ignite your personal growth

2. THE VOICE OF BENMOD TheEvolvingSpecies
Thoughts, ideas, views, and opinions to help you manage yourself in life

---

For **INTERNATIONAL** customers please get your copy from:

www.amazon.com

Or

www.createspace.com/3780005 (*The Wisdom….*)

Or

www.createspace.com/3876121

Preserving Life
C f K
Discover your purpose in life
THE CENTRE FOR KNOWLEDGE
Sowing the seeds of human development

71624001
THE CENTRE FOR KNOWLEDGE

THE CENTRE FOR KNOWLEDGE
Our Solution is Personal Development

https://sites.google.com/site/cfklife/

Made in the
USA
Middletown, DE